The Adventures of Joey

The Dog Who Barks at Puddles

Patti Holmgren

Illustrated by: Ron Croghan

ISBN 978-1-63575-482-7 (Paperback)
ISBN 978-1-63525-207-1 (Hard Cover)
ISBN 978-1-63525-206-4 (Digital)

Copyright © 2017 by Patti Holmgren

All rights reserved. No part of this publication may be reproduced, distributed, or transmitted in any form or by any means, including photocopying, recording, or other electronic or mechanical methods without the prior written permission of the publisher. For permission requests, solicit the publisher via the address below.

Christian Faith Publishing, Inc.
296 Chestnut Street
Meadville, PA 16335
www.christianfaithpublishinom

Printed in the United States of America

I dedicate this book, with love, to my friend

Herbert "Herb" F. Villemain

who inspired me to write this book.

1

My owner takes me out three times a day. I wonder what I'll see along the way. Hey look, there's a squirrel running across the yard. I think I can catch him if I run real hard. The squirrel climbed up a tree to get away from me. I followed right behind, but then, I got stuck. The squirrel climbed even higher and yelled, "Sorry, you're out of luck." They tell me dogs don't climb trees, but I didn't know, 'cause I'm just being me, you see. I've got personality.

We walked a little farther, on the sidewalk by the road, and wouldn't you know it, I saw a toad. He looked at me, and I looked at him.

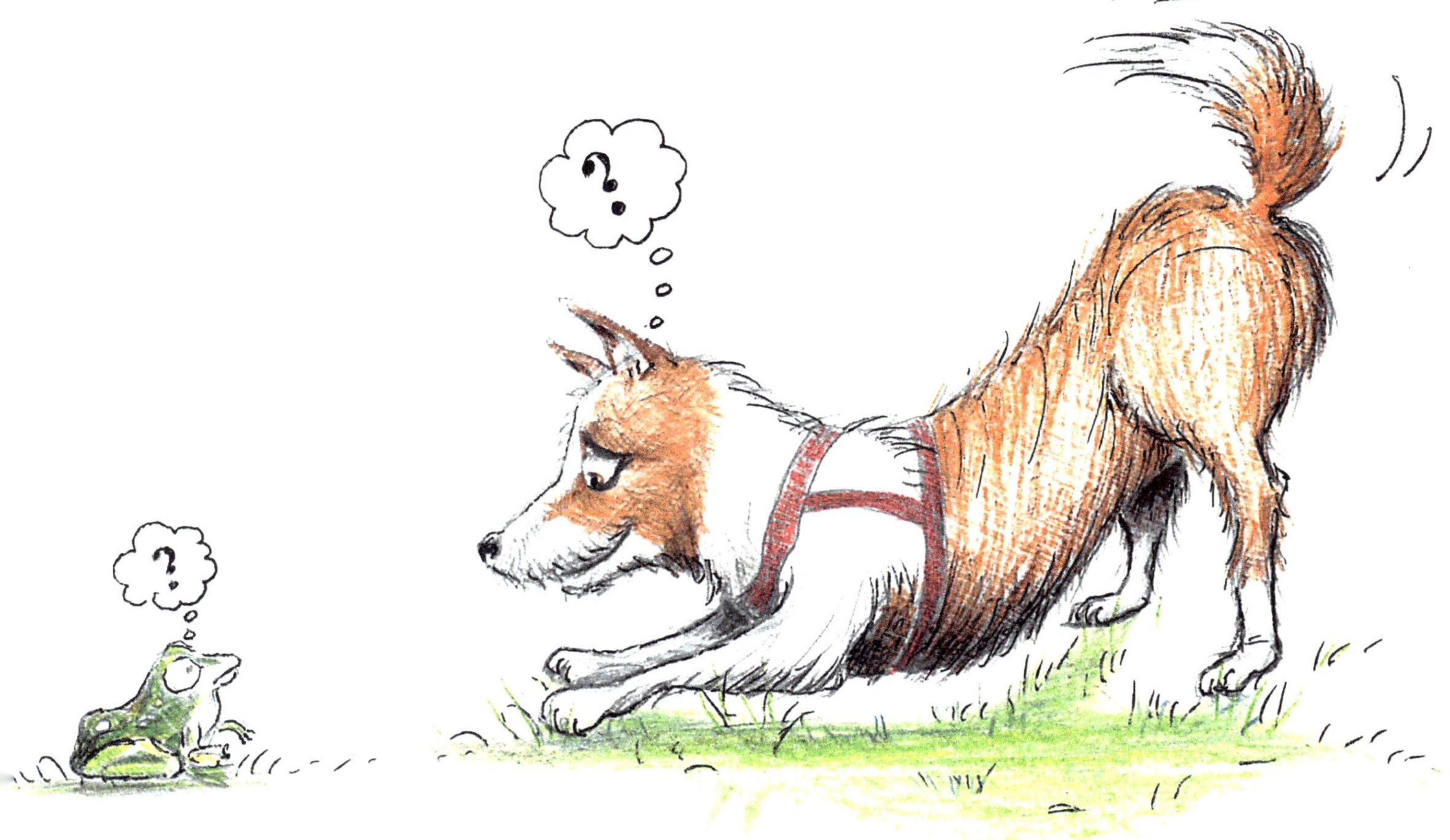

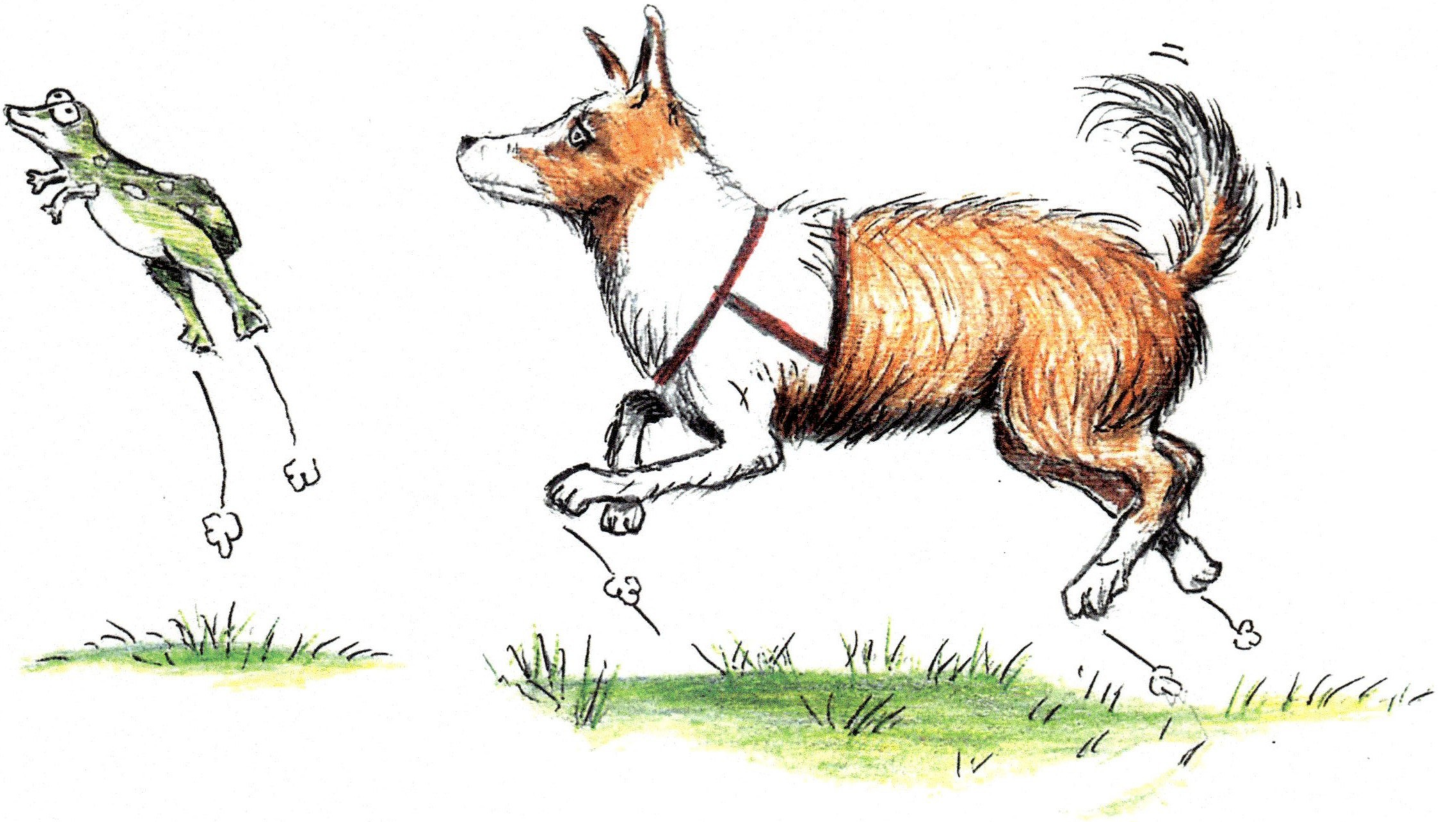

He started to hop, and I joined in. I didn't know that dogs don't hop, and even if I did, I wouldn't stop—'cause I'm just being me, you see—I've got personality.

We went back inside the house. It's not the time for me to be quiet like a mouse. I've got a bucket full of toys, and I want to play tug-of-war, even though I make lots of noise. I bring my owner my favorite toy. I pull, and she pulls, and I pull again, but I didn't win. But then, she takes the toy and throws it by the door. I run and bring it back to her, and we play some more. I then start to run, and I run back and forth, 'cause I've got lots of energy. I'm just being me, you see. I've got personality.

8

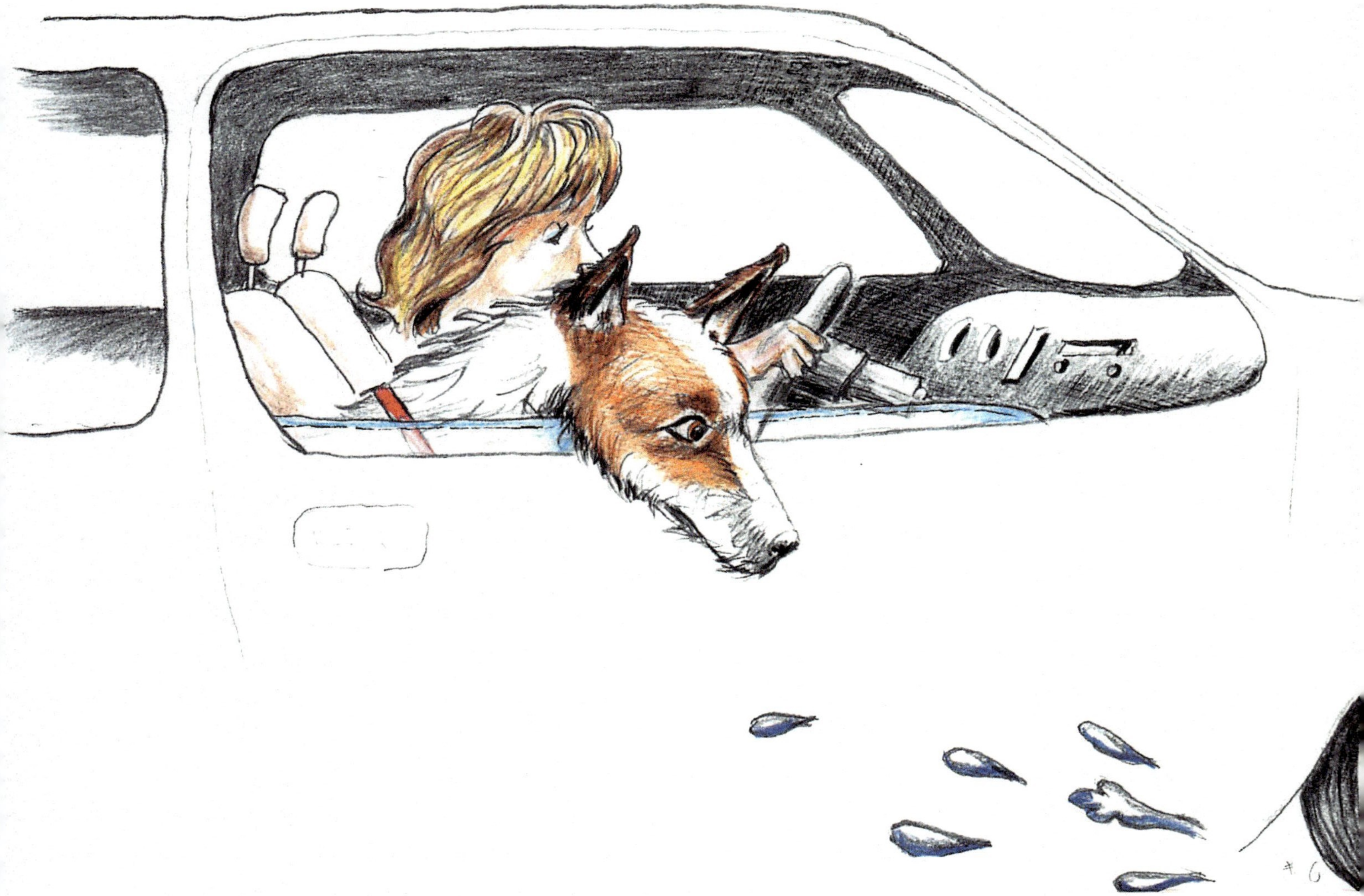

It had been raining, but the rain had stopped. It's a good thing because we have to go shop. I get to ride in the car today. While in the car, she rolls the windows down halfway. I don't know why, but I bark at puddles. The sound that it makes as the tires go through—I don't know why I bark, but I do. I stick my head out the window, and I look down at the ground. I'm curious as to why it makes that sound.

When we get home after we shop at the store, we go for another walk, and I hear it some more. Every car that goes by on the road makes that sound, and it makes me explode like a doggone hound. My owner holds tight, as I am on a rope, as I bark, and I run at the cars like a dope. I'm curious, and I bark, and I don't care who knows—'cause I'm just being me, you see. I'm a dog with personality.

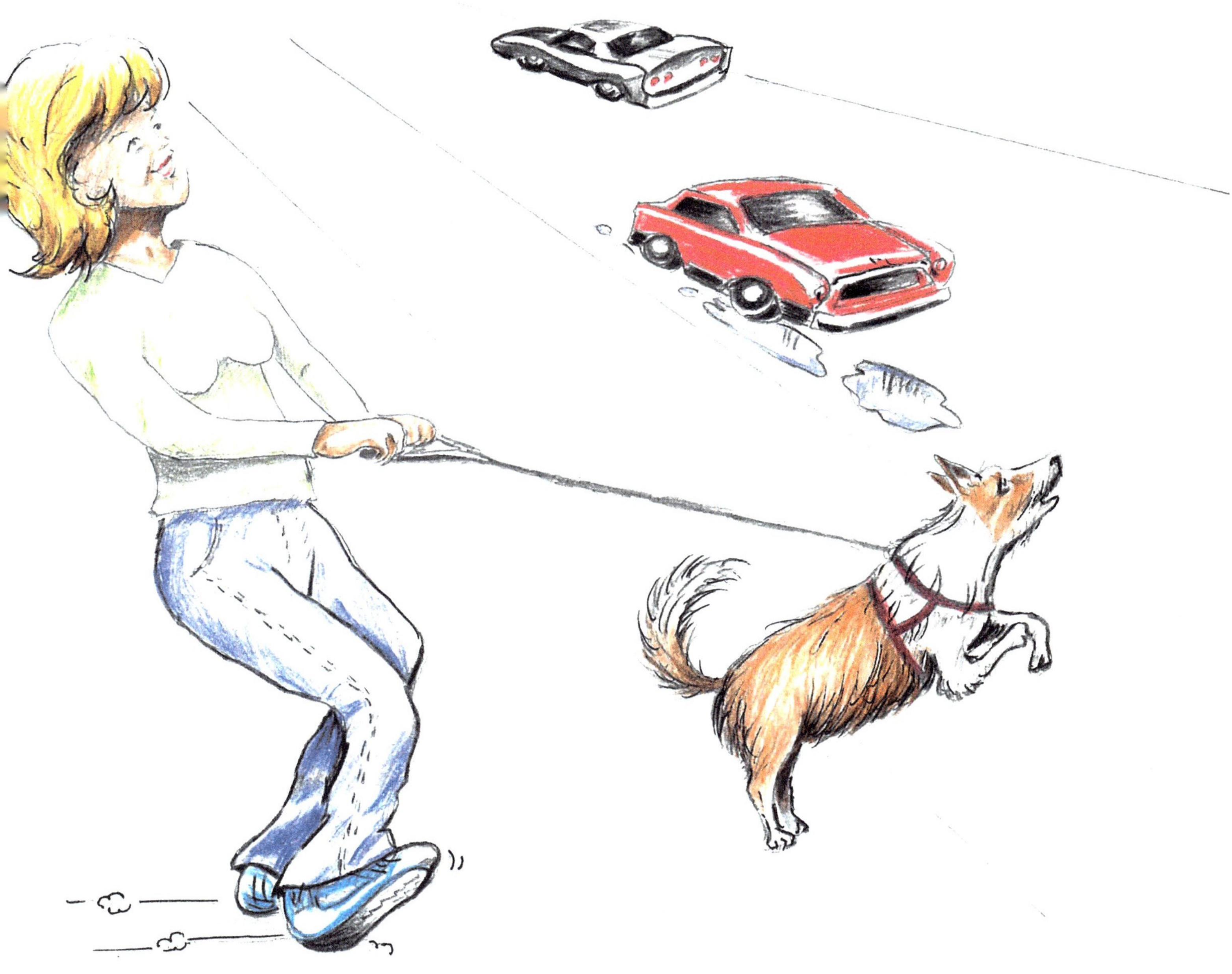

13

Dusk is approaching—one more time to go out. I know there's kids outside, 'cause I heard them shout. We got outside, and I started to run, when I heard the kids yell, "It's Joey! Now we're really going to have fun. Hey, Joey, fetch the ball, and bring it back when you hear us call."

As I rolled the ball back with the tip of my nose, I saw something move in the grass, and I froze. Then I barked, and I jumped back. Who knows, this creature may attack. He had a large, hard shell and a small, soft head. I didn't know what he was, and then the kids said, "Joey, it's a turtle. He's all right." Then the turtle tucked in his head, and he was out of sight.

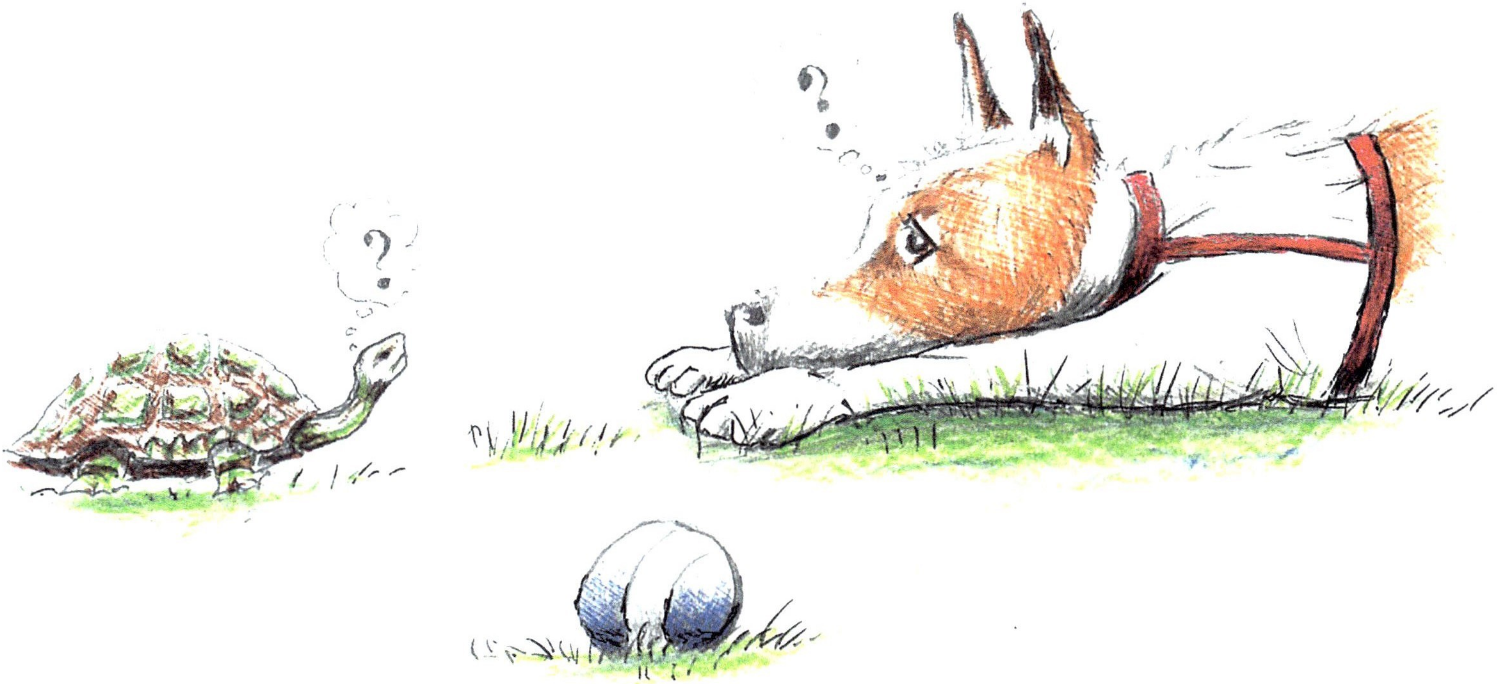

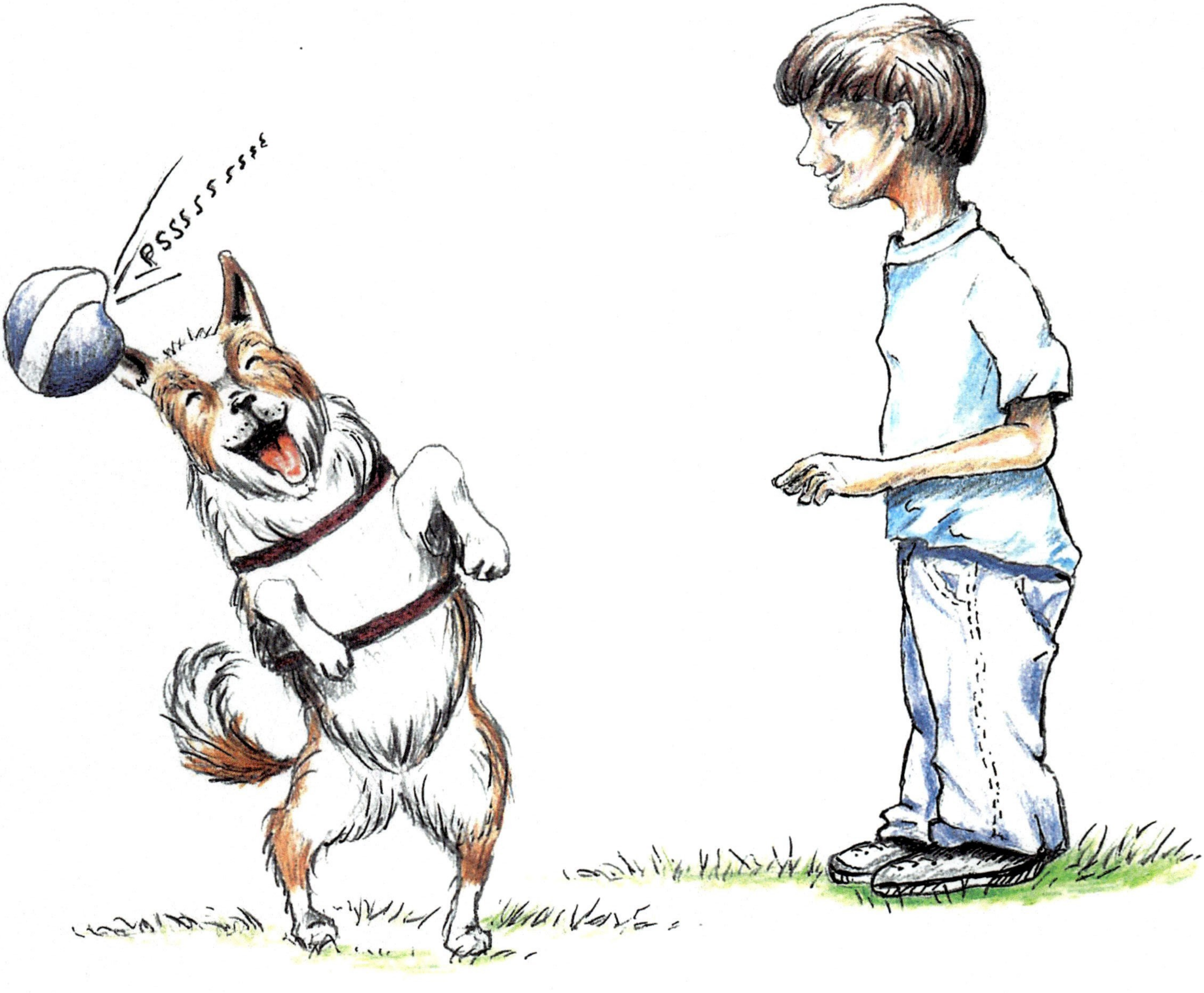
PSSSSSSS

I looked, and I saw the ball way up in the sky. I ran, and I jumped. I jumped real high. I caught the ball in my mouth and held on with my teeth. Then I heard *psssss*. The air was released. The kids could tell by my face that I looked sad, but I could tell by their voices that they weren't mad. "That's okay, Joey, that your tooth got stuck in our ball. Accidents happen, after all."

They tell me that they love me, anyway, and I'm a nice dog—they always say. I give them kisses; they pet my head, and now it's time to go to bed. Tomorrow is another day, where I can be me along life's way—'cause that's the way God meant it to be—for we all have individuality.

The End

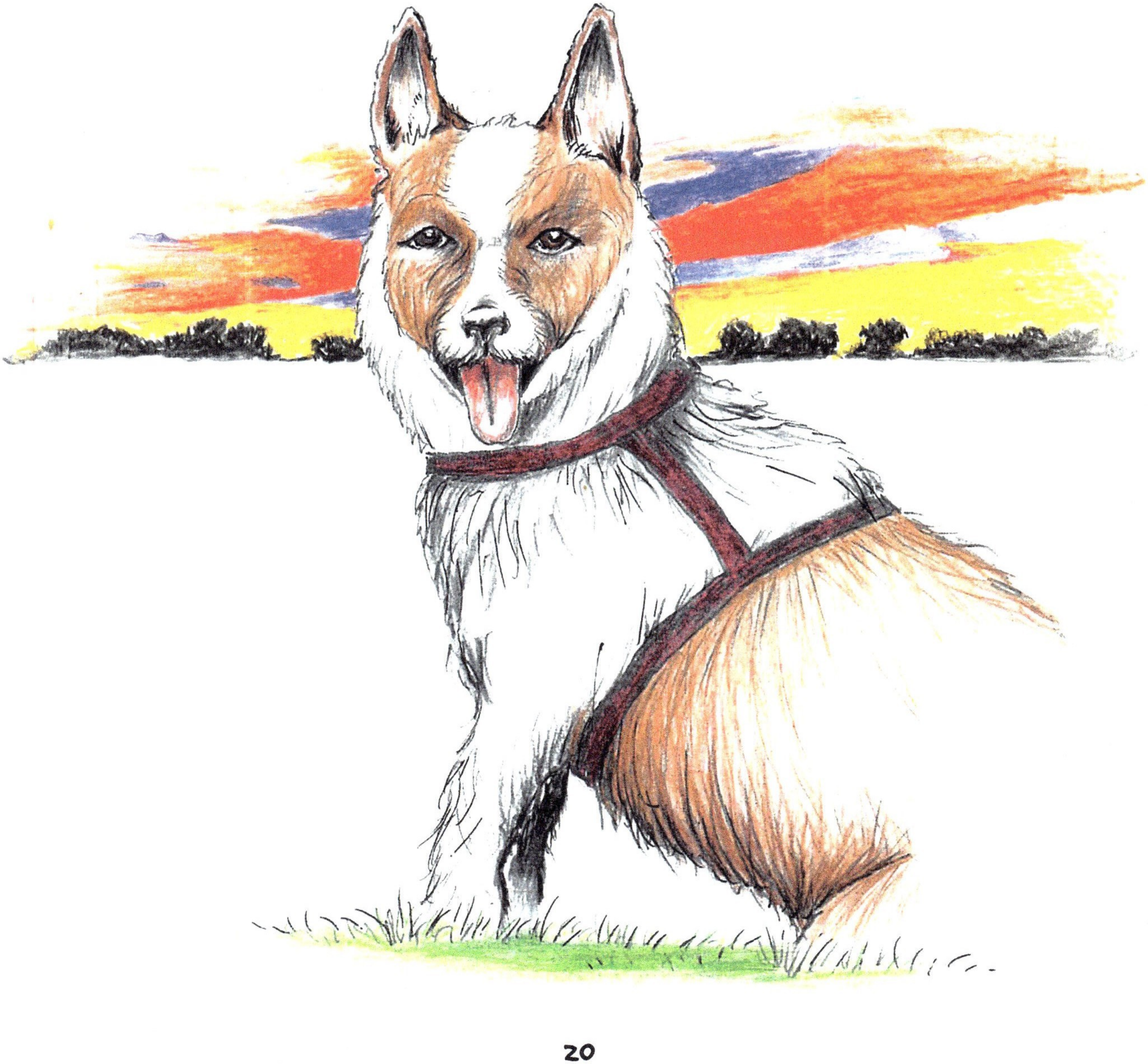

About the Author

Patti Holmgren grew up in Akron, Ohio, and graduated from Garfield High School. Although it was a nice place to grow up, at age nineteen, she, along with a friend, drove off to see the rest of the world. They went out west and had the time of their lives, especially in Kansas. Always having had an adventurous, free spirit, Patti traveled for the next three years, including going to Mexico and Hawaii for three months. In her younger years, Patti enjoyed playing sports, especially with her dad, siblings, and friends. She went skydiving a couple times down through the clouds, and then in later years, up into the clouds in a hot-air balloon with her daughter.

At age twenty-two, when Patti was done traveling, she came back to Ohio. Home is where the heart is, and the heart is where family is, so Ohio is where she got married and raised three beautiful children.

Although traveling was the most exciting time of her life, raising her three kids was the most fulfilling time of her life. It's easier to give of yourself to your family after you've had some "me time." Now, at age sixty, she is enjoying her two beautiful grandchildren and pursuing her passions, which include learning about natural supplements and writing.

Although this is her first attempt at writing a book, she did contribute a story she had written in her writing class at the library last year. At the end of class, they all put their writings into a booklet called Literary Vistas, a collected anthology from a Northeast Ohio Writer's Group. She's also written several editorials for the newspaper and various other ventures.

Patti has always had a passion for writing, especially about truth and human behavior, as it is a way to express one's deepest thoughts. Just like taking a picture of someone so that moment is never forgotten, writing keeps our thoughts in place.